The With-God Workstyle

SPIRITUAL PRACTICES FOR YOUR EOS® JOURNEY

Debbie Swindoll

The With-God Workstyle: Spiritual Practices for Your EOS® Journey
Copyright © 2022 Debbie Swindoll

First edition: August 2022

All rights reserved. No part of this book may be used or reproduced in any manner whatsoever without written permission from the publisher except in the case of brief quotations embodied in critical articles or reviews.

EOS®, EOS Process®, and Certified EOS Implementer® are registered trademarks of EOS Worldwide, LLC.

Focus Day™, Vision Building™, Level 10 Meetings™, Quarterly Pulsing™, The Accountability Chart™, Core Focus™, 10-Year Target™, 3-Year Picture™, V/TO™, The People Analyzer™, EOS Scorecard™, and The Five Leadership Abilities™ are trademarks of EOS Worldwide, LLC.

Current Strategies, LLC
2024 E. 15th Street, Suite F-384
Plano, TX 75075

Printed in the United States of America.

Editing by Curt Swindoll
Printing by IngramSpark

ISBN 13: 979-8-9867955-0-8

Table of Contents

Introduction

    How This Workbook Works *13*
    Before You Begin: A Holy Pause *16*

Spiritual Activities

    Focus Day™ *19*
    Vision Building™ Day One *25*
    Vision Building™ Day Two *31*
    Quarterly Pulsing™ *37*
    Annual Planning Meeting Preparation *51*
    Annual Planning Meeting Review *65*
    Level 10 Meetings™ *69*

Additional Resources

    Simple Spiritual Practices *74*
    An Invitation to Spiritual Direction *80*
    Recommended Reading *82*

About the Author

Introduction

EOS® is a business operating system. What intrigues many leaders is how EOS brings together best business practices in a practical framework that helps them achieve real results in a way few have experienced before.

It's a beautiful thing when the best ideas find a way to be practiced in everyday life. Often that requires some kind of structure—a framework—that holds us in activities which, over time, create habits that contribute to the outcomes we desire.

In the spiritual formation world we call that a *Rule of Life.* A Rule of Life is a set of practices or spiritual rhythms that help us grow closer to God. Often these practices provide space for us to recognize and respond to God in our daily life. Through the centuries Christians have used practices of prayer, Bible reading, meditation, personal reflection, fasting, gathering in community, etc., as a framework to regularly engage with God.

The similarity between EOS and a spiritual Rule of Life brought new life to a conversation my husband and I have engaged in for many years. The topic of that conversation: How can Christians connect more with God in their work?

Through his work with EOS and my experience in spiritual formation, we imagined how a set of spiritual practices might integrate with a set of business practices to break down the perceived tension between the business and spiritual aspects of our lives.

The result of that exploration is this workbook. If you are a Christian implementing EOS in your business or nonprofit we invite you to read on.

A Vision for a With-God Workstyle

Helping people catch a vision for how they can be *with God* in their daily activities brings great joy to my life. I love to listen to people's stories and explore how God speaks, invites, and engages with them in their circumstances. For the past decade my work as a spiritual director and curriculum developer has afforded me the privilege of walking beside others as their connection with God grows, and to witness the transformation that flows from their engagement with him.

This workbook gives me the opportunity to walk with you and explore how God desires to connect with you in your work.

What do I mean when I talk about connecting with God in your work? A conversation about integrating faith and work has been going on for some time in the church. There are several popular ways to define that integration. Here are a few you may be familiar with:

- » We live out our faith at work by working cheerfully, honoring our boss, and loving our co-workers.

- » We live out our faith at work by evangelizing our co-workers through our Christian character and our Christian witness.

- » We live out our faith at work by advancing the kingdom—we make as much as we can, so we can give as much as we can.

- » We live out our faith at work by creating something of beauty, using the gifts God gave us, and improving society.

Pause for a moment and think about how you would finish the sentence:

"I live out my faith at work by _____ ."

While there is truth in each of the examples above, there is also an inherent temptation. We can follow any of these faith/work models in our own strength, in our own wisdom, without including God in our process or execution. We can work *for* God without recognizing his presence or guidance *with* us. When I talk about "connecting with God in our work" I am referring to a relational process—a way of integrating our faith/work that puts our relationship with God at the center of our actions. When we work with God we can still achieve all of the above ends while deepening our awareness of and dependence on God.

One of the most well-known pieces of wisdom from the book of Proverbs is found in chapter three.[1]

Trust in the Lord with all your heart;
    do not depend on your own understanding.
Seek his will in all you do,
    and he will show you which path to take.
Don't be impressed with your own wisdom.
    Instead, fear the Lord and turn away from evil.
Then you will have healing for your body
    and strength for your bones.
                              Proverbs 3:5-8 (NLT)

At the core of this wisdom is a relational lifestyle, one that illustrates how to connect with God on a daily basis. This humble way of living gives us a model for how our faith can express itself in our daily work. Consider the three key actions commended in these verses.

Trust God with your whole heart. Believe that God is active and present in all your circumstances. *You are not alone in your work.*

Don't depend on your own understanding or be impressed by your own wisdom. Your experience, education or work knowledge is not the last word in your work life. *You are not on your own in your work.*

---

[1] One of the reasons these verses are treasured by many Christians is that they give us a clear and concise picture of what it looks like to walk with God in whatever we are doing. They express the same fundamental lifestyle that Jesus illustrated on earth and explained in the Gospel of John; that he only did the Father's will, not his own (John 5:19, 30; John 6:38). Jesus then goes on to tell his disciples/followers that they are meant to live that same lifestyle of connection, not living on their own but abiding with Jesus throughout their daily lives (John 15).

Seek God's will in all that you do. There is an invitation to an on-going conversation between you and God about the decisions, goals, actions, relationships, and issues that inhabit your work life. *You can seek and be with God in everything you do at work.*

Pause and consider these verses from a work perspective. What could it look like to do your work with God? How might that kind of relational connection affect your work relationships, your performance, your impact? Let me give you three benefits to consider.

*When you work with God,
you become a person of prayer.*

Many Christians have a narrow understanding and practice of prayer. Prayer can be limited to what we do in the church building, or understood as a list of requests we submit to God and wait to check off when an answer happens. Often the answer to our prayers is assumed if or when we get the thing we asked for.

But prayer is so much more than our "God, please do this for me" list. It is a foundational activity in our relationship with God. In the same way that conversation connects us in human relationships—helps us to know one another, to understand one another, to support one another—prayer connects us with God. Within that connection we can ask our questions, process our emotions, seek direction, express our doubts, look for a different perspective, find courage, learn to listen. All of these aspects of prayer help us experience the reality that God is present and we are not alone in the world.

Think about how much time you spend at work, thinking about work, maybe worrying about work. Work may occupy most of your waking hours. When you open up to the possibility of prayer (a conversation with God) intersecting those hours, prayer moves from a peripheral activity to a primary focus of your life.

How could regular conversations with God change your work experience? Here are a few possibilities.

Alleviates loneliness on the job: Often we get into the "it's all up to me" syndrome, especially if we are a leader in our business. Regular conversations with God, while we work, practically remind us that we aren't in it alone. Prayer gives us someone to turn to, to trust, to help us, and to abide with—someone who knows more than us.

Reduces the pressure you feel to perform: One of the greatest temptations of a job or career is to attach our identity to our success or performance. Doing our work within an ongoing conversation with God can regularly remind us that our core identity is found in that relationship, as a child of God, not in the outcome of our work.

Lowers your level of anxiety or worry: Work can be a stressful place with deadlines, financial ups and downs, personnel problems, etc. Stress often manifests in anxiety or worry when difficulties arise. Jesus tells us when we notice this happening it is time to connect with God—to remember his care for us. Prayer invites us into that conversation, allows us to name our fears, process them and ask for God's perspective. Over time, this relational practice can stabilize our response to stress by giving us a Person to rest in and lean on when we feel uncertain about the future.

When you work with God, work becomes a place for spiritual growth.

It is easy to think of our work life as separate from our spiritual life. When we have this mental separation, even unconsciously, we believe that we grow in our faith when we engage in overtly spiritual activities—do a Bible study, meet with our small group, attend church services—but when we work there is little opportunity to be shaped spiritually by the experience. Yet, God works in all of our circumstances to shape our lives into the image of his son. Consider these verses from Romans 8:

> *"God causes everything to work together for the good of those who love God and are called according to his purpose for them. For God knew his people in advance, and he chose them to become like his Son, so that his Son would be the firstborn among many brothers and sisters."*
>
> *Romans 8:28–29 (NLT)*

Thomas Green expresses the essence of the Apostle Paul's point in his book *Darkness in the Marketplace*. He writes, "Even in the busiest corners of our active existence, we should begin to discover that it is he who is at work always, guiding our hand to shape events and guiding events to shape our spirits."[2]

God always uses the events of our lives to invite us to grow. But, if we are oblivious to God's refining presence in our work, our growth can be stunted. God rarely miraculously changes us with no engagement from us. His usual approach invites our cooperation with his transformation plan.

Let's face it: at work, our spiritual guard is often down, which helps us observe our true character. God's refining work usually begins with the gift of clarity about ourselves. So what can this look like?

Our circumstances at work stir emotional reactions, reveal motivations, expose our lack of love toward co-workers (or competitors!), uncover our unhealthy attachment to money or success, etc. The personal reactions we experience during our work day invite us to connect with God, to talk about the deep issues of our hearts from which our actions flow. When we begin to see our work activities as means for our spiritual growth then, as Thomas Green writes, "they become for us the very sandpaper of our sanctification."[3]

This is when our work becomes spiritually exciting—a significant place of spiritual pilgrimage. Connecting with God in our work not only informs the way we behave at work but transforms the people we are at work.

---

2 Thomas H. Green, *Darkness in the Marketplace: The Christian at Prayer in the World* (Notre Dame, Ave Maria Press, 1981), 122.

3 Ibid., 121.

3

When you work with God,
you become a person of wisdom.

How do we make decisions at work? Does being a Christian influence our decision making process? The simplest answer? Being a Christian impacts our work decisions when we are guided by moral or ethical standards. While we certainly should be moral and ethical in our work, to borrow from Patrick Lencioni, this seems like a "permission-to-play" value for all Christians. What else might guide our behavior and actions and create a culture that integrates with our faith? I suggest the "something more" is to become a person of wisdom.

Timothy Keller writes, "According to the Bible, wisdom is more than just obeying God's ethical norms; it is knowing the right thing to do in the 80% of life's situations in which the moral rules don't provide the clear answer. There is no biblical law that tells you which job to take, whether to go back to school, whom to marry and befriend, when to speak out or hold your peace, whether to make the deal or walk away—yet the wrong decision can blow up your life."[4]

So what is involved in making wise decisions? When I was in grad school studying spiritual formation, we often talked about the concept of "finding the good." This phrase

---

[4] Timothy Keller, *Every Good Endeavor: Connecting Your Work to God's Work* (New York, Redeemer City, 2012), 215.

became shorthand for the process of discerning God's will in the 80% of life's situations that don't have clear answers.

We often asked each other "What's the good in this situation?" The question encouraged us to seek wisdom—to *prayerfully* discuss, listen, and explore how decisions affect others, consider what was loving, examine our motives, and try to understand where our desires and God's desires came together.

From a spiritual perspective, wisdom is more than the sum total of our business experience, our education, good business advice, gut instinct, and our passion, although many of these factors are good to consider when seeking wisdom. We find spiritual wisdom when we take all of these factors and offer them to Jesus, asking him to guide us to a solution/plan that uses these assets to accomplish his will.

Finding this kind of wisdom requires us to connect with God in our work. We must know him and ourselves well enough to be able to tell when our desires don't align with his and be willing and able to course-correct if needed. Wisdom happens in our deepening relationship with God.

In many ways becoming a person of wisdom is the by-product of being a prayerful person at work and engaging with God in how he grows us spiritually through our work. While each of these qualities affect our experience and the experience of others, being a person of wisdom has great potential to impact others in our workplace.

Wise people draw others, are sought out for advice, are regarded, are followed. True God-honoring wisdom frees us of personal agenda and empowers the greatest good which leads to our greatest success. Wisdom resonates with a deep place in the human heart that knows: there is a God and a right way to live, even if that individual is not a person of Christian faith.

Becoming a person of prayer, seeing our work as a place of spiritual pilgrimage, and developing wisdom to guide our work decisions are just three examples of what can happen when we choose to regularly connect with God in our work. I hope you are catching a vision for something exciting and transformational to your work experience. As you hold that vision in your mind, let's talk about the practical considerations to becoming such a person.

How Might We Begin to Transition to a With-God Workstyle?

We begin by considering where we find ourselves today. To be honest, we have habits of doing our work alone, in our own strength, depending on our talents, education, and experience. The more talented, experienced, and successful we are, the easier it is to *lean* on these personal resources. Our successes lead us to rarely think about or interact with God at work beyond a simple prayer for blessing on our efforts. It is only when we feel in trouble that we may turn to God to ask for wisdom or help.

Your awareness of these habits may lead to the conclusion that while this is a nice idea, maybe even the right idea, being with God in your work is impractical—impossibly at odds with your business culture. How much time might it take to include God in your work? If you are busy, perhaps struggling to "get it all done" wouldn't having to stop and talk with God about your decisions and issues grind your productivity to a halt?

Ask and explore these important questions. They give you an indication of the resistance you may feel if you decide to make changes in the way you relate with God at work. You may have had similar questions about implementing EOS. Will it be too hard to introduce EOS into our work culture? How will we find the time for session days? Will it be worth the investment of time and money? How will we get buy-in from everyone?

Depending on where you are in the EOS Process® you may still be discovering the answers to your questions. One thing you have probably already discovered, though, is that EOS has an implementation process that is guiding and holding you while these changes gradually take place. Weekly, quarterly, and annual check-points provide accountability for your progress.

Similarly, you need that kind of structure to help you gradually become the kind of person who connects with God in your work. No one goes from zero to ten overnight. This kind of spiritual transition—moving from mostly working on your own to abiding with God in your daily decisions—is a lifetime journey. You begin small and grow from there.

But, here's the good news. You can leverage EOS to create new habits of connecting with God in your work. This workbook was created to guide you in that process.

How This Workbook Works

The activities in this workbook are structured for personal engagement. Any Christian using EOS in their organization can use these activites to connect with God in their work. If you are part of a Christian leadership team or a faith-based organization you can also use this workbook to spur conversation with colleagues or build a spiritual engagement structure for your entire company.

The prayer activities coincide with your EOS session days. They invite you to engage with God around the issues and topics discussed that day. Each activity consists of guided questions and open-ended prompts that invite honest reflection and dialogue with God.

The first three exercises are post-session projects used for review after your Focus Day™ and Vision Building™ days. When you move to Quarterly Pulsing™ there are pre- and post-session exercises to prompt conversation with God as you prepare for and review each quarter. Most activities can be completed in thirty minutes to an hour.

The activity that coincides with your Annual Planning Meeting invites you to invest some extended time (about half a day) with God in preparation for those days. You will review the year and prayerfully consider where God may be leading you as you set new goals. The post-session review activity is shorter and invites you to talk with God about what happened in you and the team during your Annual meeting.

The last activity spurs prayer before and after your Level 10 Meetings™ as well as other meetings you may have. Taking five minutes before and after meetings to connect with God builds a habit of daily prayer into your schedule. These "holy pauses" in your day remind you to practice good relational skills with God and other team members. Investing five minutes at a time with God can change your perspective, responses, and relational habits at work.

All of these activities represent a place to begin and a place to experiment. Transitioning to include God in your work experience is an incremental journey. It takes time, patience and perseverance.

These practices are meant to bring peace, rest and an easy-yoke experience to your work pace. Try to avoid striving. Consider these times as a chance to take a deep breath, a long exhale, and gain some clarity with God.

There is nothing sacred or magical about the activities. I encourage you to notice what works (connects you with God) and what doesn't seem to help. Not all of the questions will seem relevant. Linger on the ones that hit home or resonate. Let God guide the process.

Don't rush. You don't need to complete the activities in a timely manner. Instead, see them as a structure to encourage you to engage with God. Once you are on the road, feel free to follow your heart and the guidance of the Spirit. Some questions may linger for days or weeks in your mind. Keep praying and listening for how God guides you to answers.

Finally, the end of this workbook outlines some simple spiritual practices to help you connect with God at work and about work. I encourage you to try the ones that intrigue you or seem helpful at different seasons of your work life. Also included is a list of additional resources for your enjoyment and growth. If you have feedback or questions about how you can use this workbook in your company, feel free to contact me at *debbie@currentstrategies.com*

I trust God to guide you in this process and give you an experience of his love and grace along the way.

Debbie Swindoll, Spiritual Integration
Current Strategies

BEFORE YOU BEGIN

A Holy Pause

In my work as a spiritual director (see the back of this workbook for a definition of spiritual direction) I often say to my directees at the end of a session, "We have talked about a lot of things; you need to take what we have talked about and have further conversation with God."

I know from experience: when God's children recognize God's voice within a conversation, when they discern how the Holy Spirit is directing them through what was said, there is more power and "stickiness" for them to follow through.

Before you make a decision about using this workbook, I invite you to take some time and talk with God about what you have read. Reconsider Proverbs 3:5-8:

> *Trust in the Lord with all your heart;*
> > *do not depend on your own understanding.*
> *Seek his will in all you do,*
> > *and he will show you which path to take.*
> *Don't be impressed with your own wisdom.*
> > *Instead, fear the Lord and turn away from evil.*
> *Then you will have healing for your body*
> > *and strength for your bones.*
> > > > *Proverbs 3:5-8 (NLT)*

Do you sense an invitation from God in these verses? Do you see new ways you might engage with God in your work?

What resonated with you as you read this introduction? Ask God if this resonance was a prompting of the Spirit.

Ask God what he would like for you to do with this workbook. Spend some time over the next few days listening for an answer.

Focus Day™

*Commit your actions to the Lord,
and your plans will succeed.*
                              Proverbs 16:3 (NLT)

Once you have completed Focus Day, you have officially begun the EOS Process. You are excited and a little daunted by the number of practices you are learning and implementing. That is normal. Building skills takes time but is worth the effort. Breaking your old meeting habits will bring clarified focus. Honestly talking about your real issues will breathe fresh life into your organization.

How might you be with God as you transition into these new ways to lead?

First, talk with God when you feel frustrated or overwhelmed by learning something new. Change stirs up emotions—like resistance, hope, impatience, fear for the future, mistrust between team members, resentment, grief over letting go of the past, doubt about personal capacities. You and your team are being stretched and challenged in new ways.

From a spiritual perspective, this is a good thing. Emerging feelings, especially those that you are surprised by, give you an opportunity to notice internal dynamics within the company and within yourself. Naming and processing these emotions is an opportunity for spiritual growth individually and as a team if you include God in your conversations.

Second, Talk with God if it doesn't all come together immediately. The Focus Day Tools you are implementing will be refined over time. It is not unusual for an organization to make changes to their Accountability Chart™ and EOS Scorecard™ in the first few weeks and months. EOS has given you a chance to look at your operations with fresh eyes and to talk honestly about personnel and processing issues. You will discover things that are working and things that still need to evolve. Ask God for wisdom as you navigate and refine the process.

Use the following spiritual activity to process and pray through your observations.

SPIRITUAL ACTIVITY

Focus Day Reflection

Set aside some time to be alone with God. Find a place where you will not be disturbed. Put away any devices that will distract you. There is space provided below to make notes.

Begin your time with some quiet. Notice the thoughts that are running through your mind. Ask God to help you set those aside for a while. Pay attention to how your body is feeling—do you notice tension or pain anywhere? Purposefully relax your muscles and settle into your chair.

Turn your attention to God. He is present with you in this exercise. Renew your mind with these thoughts:

» *God has been present with you during this implementation of EOS whether you have recognized his presence or not.*

» *God understands every dynamic that has happened on your team so far.*

» *God sees internal realities—in you and in your team members—that you have not noticed and can not understand.*

» *God desires to use everything that has happened and is happening to shape you into the image of his Son.*

Ask God to help you as you reflect and process your observations, questions and personal emotions which are surfacing through the EOS practices.

Use the following questions as prompts for reflection:

✎ What excites you as you begin the EOS journey?

- What are you hoping will happen as a result of this implementation?

- Do you have any skepticism about the success of EOS in your environment?

- Have you noticed any resistance in yourself or others on your team as a result of the EOS tools that you are practicing: Running L10 meetings? Keeping Scorecard metrics? Accountability Chart changes?

- Have you felt any discouragement or confusion in making these changes?

- Have you been able to be more honest with one another on the leadership team? If so, how has that been received by everyone? If not, where do you sense resistance to being more open and honest?

- What is the most positive change that you have experienced?

✎ Has anything happened that is causing you concern?

Now, look over your answers. Talk with God about those that stand out to you, both good and bad:

Ask God what he might be doing in each of these circumstances to grow you and your leadership team.

Seek God's perspective in situations where you feel stuck or unsure of how to proceed.

Ask for God's help in any relationships that are strained through this process. How might you grow in love as a team?

Thank God for the progress you have made. Name ways that you have seen him assist you and your team in the process.

Vision Building™

Day One

Trust in the Lord with all your heart;
   do not depend on your own understanding.
Seek his will in all you do,
   and he will show you which path to take.
                              Proverbs 3:5-6 (NLT)

When you begin the process of building your Vision/Traction Organizer™, excitement comes from stepping back and looking at the potential of your organization. Naming or revisiting your Core Values, seeing the possibilities of the People Analyzer™, narrowing down your Core Focus™ and Niche, all remind us why we love the work that we do.

Through this process you are growing in your understanding of how each team member contributes to your success. You are evaluating "right people, right seats" and honoring the unique giftedness represented in yourselves and your employees. You are envisioning where this team could go in the future given your talents and potential.

Now is a good time to ask:

» how God might be inviting you to include him in your plans.

> » what it could look like to be with God in this process.
> » if God desires to contribute something beyond your collective talents.

The following spiritual activity will help you consider these questions and talk with God about what you want, and listen for what he wants. You can engage in the exercise as an individual or as a team. Give yourself time to reflect and notice what is happening around you and in you as you ponder the questions. Consider spreading the questions over several days. Whatever time you give God in this process will not be wasted.

SPIRITUAL ACTIVITY

V/TO™ Day One Reflection

If you are doing this project as an individual, set aside some time to be alone with God. Find a place where you will not be disturbed. Put away any devices that will distract you. Have some paper handy to make notes.

If you are doing this project in community, consider going off site where you will be away from your normal interruptions. Allow time for individuals to answer the questions for themselves and then share your thoughts with one another. Take pauses for quiet and prayer, making room for God to speak within your meeting. Listen well. Don't interrupt, interpret or judge each other when one of you is sharing. Value the honest answer. Ask clarifying questions. Encourage and affirm one another.

As you begin, stop for a minute and be with God in the excitement you feel from your first vision day. Thank him for the gift of good work. Tell him what you enjoy and what you are looking forward to in your job. Remember that God created good works for you to walk in.

Ask God to help you listen to him as you ponder these questions. Pause and open your awareness to God's presence with you, his love for you, his kind thoughts toward you.

Read the wisdom expressed in Proverbs 3.

> *Trust in the Lord with all your heart;*
> *　do not depend on your own understanding.*
> *Seek his will in all you do,*
> *　and he will show you which path to take.*
> *　　　　　　　　　　　　Proverbs 3:5-6 (NLT)*

✎ What are your initial thoughts about how this wisdom applies to your position at work?

✎ What are your initial thoughts about how this wisdom could apply to your team?

- Review the Core Values you identified for your organization. Pause on each one and talk with God about why you see each value as important. Ask God if he has anything to say about these values. Make a note of any thoughts, impressions or Scriptures that come to mind.

- Reflect on your work within the organization. Are you living into each of these values? Where might there be room for improvement? How might you be with God as you move toward deeper integration of these values in your work?

- Reflect on the people who work under you. Do they exhibit these Core Values? Talk with God about how you might encourage them to grow in these areas.

- Review your Core Focus and Niche. Talk with God about your emotional response to these statements. Notice if you are enlivened by this focus. Does it touch a spiritual core inside of you?

- Ask God what he thinks about your focus. Is pursuing this work in line with God's plans for your life right now? Make a note of any thoughts that influence your answer.

- As you consider spending your days pursuing your Core Focus, how do you need God's help in the process? In what ways might you continue to dialogue with God about his will as you work?

✏ Ask God if he has any additional thoughts regarding your VB1 session day. Make a note of whatever comes to mind.

Vision Building™

Day Two

Trust in the Lord with all your heart;
    do not depend on your own understanding.
Seek his will in all you do,
    and he will show you which path to take.
                    Proverbs 3:5-6 (NLT)

Congratulations! You have now finished building your Vision/Traction Organizer™. This simple document provides clarity for your team and focuses your actions. This may be the first time you feel hopeful that your strategic plan can become a reality. You have your 3-Year Picture™, your 1-Year Plan, and your Rocks set for the quarter. You also have tools in place to keep you accountable to your progress along the way.

How are you feeling? Are you energized for the future? A little nervous about getting it all done? Hopeful about this process and how it might bring healthier habits to your team? Still a little worried that real change can be sustained by all?

How can you be with God as you process your thoughts and feelings?

The following spiritual activity will help you talk with God about your thoughts and observations, post VB2. You can engage in the activity as an individual or as a team. Give yourself time to reflect and notice what is happening around you and in you as you ponder the questions. Whatever time you give God in this process will not be wasted.

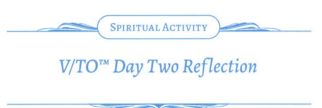

V/TO™ Day Two Reflection

» *If you are doing this project as an individual,* set aside some time to be alone with God. Find a place where you will not be disturbed. Put away any devices that will distract you. Have some paper handy to make notes.

» *If you are doing this project in community,* consider going off site where you will be away from your normal interruptions. Allow time for individuals to answer the questions for themselves and then share your thoughts with one another. Take pauses for quiet and prayer, making room for God to speak within your meeting. Listen well. Don't interrupt, interpret or judge each other when one of you is sharing. Value the honest answer. Ask clarifying questions. Encourage and affirm one another.

As you begin, enter into a short time of silence. Pay attention to your body, your breath, your heart beat. Acknowledge God's presence with you. Tell him what you are thankful for. Enter into a short time of worship—quietly lifting your hands, listening to a worship song, praising God for his attributes, feeling your love for one another. Ask God to help you listen to him as you ponder these questions.

Revisit the wisdom expressed in Proverbs 3:

> *Trust in the Lord with all your heart;*
> *do not depend on your own understanding.*
> *Seek his will in all you do,*
> *and he will show you which path to take.*
> *Proverbs 3:5-6 (NLT)*

- How have you experienced God in your work in the last 30 days? When have you been sensitive to God's will? When have you been oblivious to God and operated in your own understanding?

- If your LT is engaging in this spiritual exercise together, consider how you have experienced God's leadership and presence on your team in the last 30 days. When has the team been in tune with God together? When has God been ignored or not considered in your times together?

- ✎ Have you noticed any difference in the times when you remembered God and the times when you were operating in your own understanding? What were the results?

- ✎ Review your 10-Year Target™ and your 3-Year Picture. Talk with God about what excites you about these plans. Tell him what makes you nervous, anxious or concerned.

- ✎ Ask God if he has anything to say about these plans. Make a note of any thoughts, impressions or Scriptures that come to mind.

- Review your 1-Year Plan and the Rocks that you are responsible for this quarter. Talk with God about your thoughts and feelings related to your plan and work load.

- What kinds of spiritual activities could keep you connected with God as you execute these goals? Consider for example:

    » Morning prayer at your desk
    » Two or three pauses during the day to be attentive to God, seek his will and talk about your responses to work issues
    » An evening review (*examen*) with God to go over your day
    » A short noon prayer time with a colleague to lift your organization before God

- Consider setting a personal spiritual Rock for this quarter—something tangible that you can do to grow in your attentiveness to God while you work. Talk this over with God. Then share your Rock with someone in your life or someone on your team to check in with you to see how you are doing.

End your time by rereading Proverbs 3:5-6. Thank God that he wants to be with you in everything that you do.

Quarterly Pulsing™

*People may be right in their own eyes,
but the Lord examines their heart.*
Proverbs 21:2 (NLT)

Quarterly meetings are designated times to assess our progress and set new Rocks as an organization. The rhythm of our quarterly meetings is also a good time to spiritually reflect and review our relationship with God.

Use the prompts in these activities to consider your work with God. There is space provided to make notes. (You will see that these activities repeat for future quarterly pulsing.)

SPIRITUAL ACTIVITY

Quarterly Meeting Preparation

SESSION DATE:

✎ Look over your current EOS Scorecard™ and quarterly Rocks—what are you feeling, what are you thankful for, what are you anxious about?

✎ If you are off-track with your Rocks, talk with God about the situation. Ask for his perspective. Talk with him about any emotions, frustrations, etc. that you are feeling.

- If you are on-track with your Rocks, consider if God has been present in your success. Have you achieved your goals through steady perseverance with God or in striving on your own?

- Where have you seen God at work this quarter—in you, in your colleagues, in your clients/customers? Consider both successes, frustrations or conflicts. How have you responded to what God has done?

SPIRITUAL ACTIVITY

Quarterly Meeting Review

SESSION DATE:

✐ Review the meeting in your mind. Talk with God about what you are thankful for, what surprised you and anything you are concerned about moving forward. Ask for his perspective.

✐ Look at your Rocks for the next 90 days. How might you persevere to accomplish these objectives while leaving the ultimate outcome in God's hands?

✐ What spiritual practices might you need to keep you connected with God as you pursue these goals—prayer, reflection, time alone, community engagement, spiritual direction/counsel, etc.?

SPIRITUAL ACTIVITY

Quarterly Meeting Preparation

SESSION DATE:

- Look over your current EOS Scorecard™ and quarterly Rocks—what are you feeling, what are you thankful for, what are you anxious about?

- If you are off-track with your Rocks, talk with God about the situation. Ask for his perspective. Talk with him about any emotions, frustrations, etc. that you are feeling.

- If you are on-track with your Rocks, consider if God has been present in your success. Have you achieved your goals through steady perseverance with God or in striving on your own?

- Where have you seen God at work this quarter—in you, in your colleagues, in your clients/customers? Consider both successes, frustrations or conflicts. How have you responded to what God has done?

Spiritual Activity

Quarterly Meeting Review

Session Date:

- Review the meeting in your mind. Talk with God about what you are thankful for, what surprised you and anything you are concerned about moving forward. Ask for his perspective.

- Look at your Rocks for the next 90 days. How might you persevere to accomplish these objectives while leaving the ultimate outcome in God's hands?

- What spiritual practices might you need to keep you connected with God as you pursue these goals—prayer, reflection, time alone, community engagement, spiritual direction/counsel, etc.?

SPIRITUAL ACTIVITY

Quarterly Meeting Preparation

SESSION DATE:

- Look over your current EOS Scorecard™ and quarterly Rocks—what are you feeling, what are you thankful for, what are you anxious about?

- If you are off-track with your Rocks, talk with God about the situation. Ask for his perspective. Talk with him about any emotions, frustrations, etc. that you are feeling.

- If you are on-track with your Rocks, consider if God has been present in your success. Have you achieved your goals through steady perseverance with God or in striving on your own?

- Where have you seen God at work this quarter—in you, in your colleagues, in your clients/customers? Consider both successes, frustrations or conflicts. How have you responded to what God has done?

Spiritual Activity

Quarterly Meeting Review

Session Date:

- Review the meeting in your mind. Talk with God about what you are thankful for, what surprised you and anything you are concerned about moving forward. Ask for his perspective.

- Look at your Rocks for the next 90 days. How might you persevere to accomplish these objectives while leaving the ultimate outcome in God's hands?

✎ What spiritual practices might you need to keep you connected with God as you pursue these goals—prayer, reflection, time alone, community engagement, spiritual direction/counsel, etc.?

Annual Planning Meeting

Preparation

Don't copy the behavior and customs of this world, but let God transform you into a new person by changing the way you think. Then you will learn to know God's will for you, which is good and pleasing and perfect.
Romans 12:2 (NLT)

As you anticipate your Annual Planning Meeting, set aside half a day to be alone with God. Consider going to a local retreat center, park or similar venue that offers you quiet space for reflection and prayer. If the weather permits it can be helpful to choose a place where you can get up and walk during your mini retreat.

Wear comfortable clothes, and bring the following:

» any reports/statistics that help you reflect on the activities and results in your organization in the last year
» your Bible
» paper and pen to record your observations, thoughts, and questions

Don't bring anything that will distract you from your focus for the day.

We have structured this guided, spiritual activity into three sections: time to look back, time to look within, and time to look forward. Questions will offer prompts for reflection and prayer. If you get stuck, get tired, or feel frustrated, get up and move around for a while. Pay attention to what you notice while you walk. Let questions percolate a bit if you don't have an answer. Feel free to skip ahead and come back to a question later or to simply sit quietly with God for a few minutes.

Remember that God is with you in this time away. He has things he wants you to notice about him, about yourself and about your organization. There aren't "right" answers to the questions, there are only honest answers that help you connect with God and yourself in truth.

SPIRITUAL ACTIVITY

Annual Planning Meeting Preparation

As you arrive, acclimate to your setting. Walk around for a few minutes. Get the lay of the land. Pray a prayer of blessing on the facility and your time there. Find a comfortable place to settle in for reflection and prayer. Take some deep breaths. Acknowledge God. Ask for wisdom.

Then begin when you feel you have cleared your mind enough to have space to reflect and pray.

1. Time to Review

Get out any reports that you have brought along regarding the activity in your organization in the last year—Scorecard data, Rock achievements, financial reports, personnel information, your Vision/Traction Organizer etc.

Look at all the numbers, progress, and statistics that express the state of your organization.

✎ What is the first thing you notice?

✎ What is the first emotion that you feel?

- Explore your initial reaction with God.

Look over the information again, this time at a slower, more prayerful pace. Talk with God about your questions. Ask for his perspective on what you are noticing and feeling.

- What do you see this time that you missed the first time through? Has your emotional reaction to the information changed in any way?

- Make a list of the significant events in your organization in the last year, both good and seemingly bad. For example: personnel changes, client changes, financial upturns or downturns, goals achieved, milestones met, redirections, losses or disappointments.

    » What do you think are the three most important events of the last year?

- » How did you experience God in or around these events?
- » What did you learn?
- » How did these events affect your organization? Your people? Yourself?
- » Ask God if there is anything else he wants you to know, see or understand about these events.

✎ What do you want to remember about these events as you move forward? Talk with God about your answer. Ask for his perspective on what you should remember and what you should accept and leave behind.

Take a short break to walk around and clear your head before you start the next section.

2. Time for Personal Assessment

Prayerfully consider these questions with God:

- Has your work this last year been energizing and challenging?

- Have you worked in your core giftedness or outside of your sweet spot?

- What functions have drained your energy?

✎ How would you describe your work/life balance?

✎ What do you notice about your physical health? Has your job hindered your health in any way? Has your health hindered your job in any way?

✎ Have you had time for rest and rejuvenation this last year?

✏️ How would you describe your personal state as you begin this next year at work:

- » Physically
- » Mentally
- » Emotionally
- » Spiritually
- » Relationally

Talk with God about any areas of your life that seem unhealthy or unready to begin a new year.

✏️ How has God used your work this last year to grow you spiritually?

🖊 In what areas would you like to see God more clearly in your work?

🖊 Are there issues at work in which you could use more wisdom? Ask God for what you need.

End your time of personal assessment by asking God if there is anything you need to change about the way you work this next year to live a healthier life, a life more honoring to him, more loving and more connected with him.

Take a short break to walk around and clear your head before you start the next section.

3. Time to Look Ahead

Prayerfully consider these questions with God:

✎ What are you looking forward to in this next year at work? What excites you about your organization?

✎ What are your personal goals for this next year at work?

✎ What would be disappointing if it didn't happen this next year?

- Where would you like to grow in your skills and contribution to the organization?

- What would you like to see God do that would be beyond your capabilities?

- How might God want to use your organization in this next year to advance his kingdom?

✎ How might God want to use your job to grow you spiritually?

✎ How might your work be a place where you grow in love for God and others?

✎ Are there spiritual practices that you would like to add this next year to your workflow?

As you anticipate your annual meeting:

✎ What do you want to ask God for?

✎ How might you remember to be present to God during the meeting?

Pray specifically for each colleague that will be at the annual meeting. Ask God to bless them. Ask for discernment, for wisdom and for God's will to be done.

Make a note of any impressions that you received from your time of prayer.

Annual Planning Meeting

Review

So we have not stopped praying for you since we first heard about you. We ask God to give you complete knowledge of his will and to give you spiritual wisdom and understanding. Then the way you live will always honor and please the Lord, and your lives will produce every kind of good fruit. All the while, you will grow as you learn to know God better and better.
Colossians 1:9-10 (NLT)

After you have completed your Annual Planning Meeting, set aside some time to talk with God. Reflect on the following questions as you pray.

- Look over your notes from the session. What excites you about this next year?

- Is there anything that causes you concern? If so, ask for God's perspective on the issue.

- As you consider your yearly plan, what would you like to pray for this year? Might this be something that you pray together as a team?

✎ Look at your Rocks for the next 90 days. What spiritual practices do you need in order to persevere to accomplish these objectives while leaving the ultimate outcome in God's hands?

Level 10 Meetings™

Scheduled meetings can remind you to connect with God throughout the day. The following short prayers (about 5 minutes) will help you be with God as you participate in Level 10 meetings. They can be used before and after other meetings as well.

SPIRITUAL ACTIVITY

Meeting Preparation

"Lord, in this moment I remember that you are always present with me. Help me to be present with you as I engage in this meeting."

"Help me to look for your will above my own."

» Be honest with God about any personal agenda that you are bringing into this meeting. Ask God to help you evaluate your desires in light of his will.

- » Express to God any personal need or problem that is playing on your mind. Ask God to meet your needs, in his time and perfect will.

"Help me to be present with others with honesty and love."

- » Picture the faces of the people you will be interacting with in this meeting. Thank God for the gift of these colleagues.

- » Acknowledge if there are any personal struggles or conflicts with any of these people. Talk with God about these struggles. Ask God for wisdom as you interact with others and make decisions.

Notes

SPIRITUAL ACTIVITY

Meeting Review

"Lord, I ask for your perspective and guidance as I reflect on what happened in my meeting. I desire to grow in my love for you and in my love for this team."

"Help me recall what I saw and heard that I should remember."

- » Reflect on the ideas, thoughts or suggestions which came to light in the meeting. Do any seem more significant than others? Is God guiding you through this idea?

- » Recall the tone of the conversations. Did the dialogue honor people—their perspective and contribution? Was it honest and loving?

"Help me recall how I acted, reacted and responded during the meeting."

- » Explore with God both positive and negative responses that come to mind.

- » Talk with God about any emotions that you felt during the meeting which may have influenced your actions. Thank God for the times when you felt in unity with the Spirit.

"Help me understand what I need to follow up on."

» Did you become aware of a personal issue you need to explore with Jesus or others?

» Did you become aware of another person's need or a company issue that requires prayer, more discussion or further action?

» Ask God for guidance on where you go from here.

✎ *Notes*

Additional Resources

One of The Five Leadership Abilities™ that help organizations break through ceilings—take their businesses to the next level—is the ability to simplify. Rooting out complexity to find the handful of practices that produce consistent results helps facilitate consistent movement toward our goals. When a process feels complex, burdensome, or confusing, it can derail participation from the start.

Keeping that principle in mind, I offer you a handful of spiritual exercises that are simple to execute, time efficient, and highly effective in growing your relationship with God.

As you look over these suggestions, pay attention to what seems realistic. While the practices themselves are easy, consistency is important. Be practical. Try one at a time to give yourself the best chance for follow-through. Consider making your choice a quarterly Rock and evaluate your experience after 90 days. Overtime, notice which practices enhance your relationship and connection with God at work. When you find something helpful, make that practice a part of your regular work rhythm.

Simple Spiritual Practices

The Daily Examen

The idea of a daily examen comes from Ignatius of Loyola, a spiritual leader from the 16th century. At its core, the examen is a 15 minute practice that helps us reflect on our day, notice where God was active, and how we responded to God and others in our activities.

The examen is practiced once or twice a day at a convenient time, often at noon and/or at the end of the day. It provides a simple structure to look back over what happened, connect with God, and then look forward to what may happen tomorrow and seek God's guidance and help.

If you want to explore a daily examen I recommend Mark Thibodaux's book, Reimagining the Ignatian Examen. Thibodaux's approach is simple, accessible, and easy to follow. You can see a structure for the examen at *Reimagining the Ignatian Examen* by Mark E. Thibodeaux, SJ (*ignatianspirituality.com*). You will also find an examen prayer app to download for your phone or tablet.

Schedule Appointments with God

Calendars are great tools to remind you to connect with God. Look over your schedule at the beginning of the week. Identify two or three short windows (15 minute time slots) when you can take a break with God. Put an appointment on your calendar to meet with God at those times. Resist the temptation to push these appointments aside for other, seemingly pressing work. Trust that God can keep you effective if you spend these moments with him.

When your appointment with God arrives, keep it simple but take it seriously. Silence your phone and shut down email or texts. Be present to God.

Here are a few suggestions to try:

- » If something is on your mind or you feel anxious, tell God about it.
- » If you feel the need to get out of the office, take a short walk with God.
- » If you could use quiet, sit silently with God. Notice your breathing. Ask God to refresh you.
- » If you need help focusing, play a couple worship songs and let them lead you to connection with God.
- » If you feel discouraged, make a list of 5 things you are grateful for and express your thanksgiving to God.

Practice Listening in Prayer

Many leaders listen poorly and poor listeners generally have shallow relationships with both people and God. In order to make progress in connecting with God at work, increase your capacity to listen.

Consider these three ways to practice listening in prayer.

Schedule 5 minutes of silence into your day.

Set a timer. During this time be mindful of God's presence. Let mental distractions go. Breathe deeply. It might be helpful to place your hands in your lap in an open posture of receiving. Begin with Samuel's words, "Speak Lord, your servant is listening."

Remember that the point of this exercise is better listening skills. If you do not" hear" anything from God, don't worry. Focus on your availability to God and reducing your internal noise to become present with him. Often the busyness in our minds keeps us from hearing God. Over time this practice grows your capacity to quiet your thoughts to create space to receive and truly hear what God has to say.

Practice listening to others in your meetings and conversations.

Leaders can use meetings and conversations with others at work merely as a means to get their point across. Healthy leaders listen well, ask good follow-up questions, and seek to truly understand their colleague's viewpoints or ideas.

If we listen poorly to others it has ramifications in our relationship with them. But it also affects our relationship with God because God can speak to us through the words of others. Conversely, listening well to others expresses our love for them and deepens our connection with God when we open our hearts to what he might be saying to us through these conversations. When this happens our dialogues with others can become a form of prayer.

To grow your listening skills with others, consider these suggestions:

» Let others talk first. Give them your undivided attention.

» Don't respond to what others have shared until you understand what they are trying to communicate. Ask follow-up questions to clarify their meaning.

» Express appreciation for what others share. Welcome honesty.

» After you share, invite others to respond. Be open to their feedback.

» After the conversation, ask God if he was communicating something to you through what was shared. Spend a few minutes listening with God as you review what you heard.

3

Practice listening to yourself.

One of the ways God speaks to us is through internal experiences—our thoughts, deep impressions, inner peace, or a still, small voice. Understanding God's communication requires awareness of our internal state and the ability to distinguish between God's voice and our own.

Learning to discern God's voice within requires a specific kind of listening in prayer. We need to develop a capacity for listening to ourselves and talking with God about what we hear.

Here are some suggestions about how you can practice listening to yourself and grow in your capacity to discern.

- » Acknowledge your emotional reactions. Be honest when something triggers you and you act out of an emotion. Process your feelings with God. Ask him to help you discover what lies beneath the emotion.

- » Listen to your stress levels. Identify where you feel stress. For example, does stress show up in your back, tight shoulders, a headache in your forehead, a stomach ache, etc. When you know how your body expresses stress you can listen for when it happens. Take your stress into a conversation with God to see if it is motivating your actions or clouding your judgment.

» Listen to your body beyond where it holds stress. Evaluate your energy levels, your weariness, even the color of your skin and whether your face looks refreshed or haggard. Your body can tell you a lot if you pay attention. As you notice the state of your body, talk with God about what you observe, what it means, and how he would like for you to respond to the condition of your body.

» Pay attention to your instincts and gut responses. God can use our intuition to lead us—a deep sense of peace and freedom, or caution—but our intuition also responds to personal fears and habits of self-protection. We need conversations with God to help us distinguish how or if God is using our gut to guide our decisions.

» Listen to recurring thoughts. Some recurring thoughts are like old tapes from our childhood that create a familiar soundtrack. But recurring thoughts can also be the Holy Spirit trying to get our attention. Either way, these thoughts invite us to connect with God, to seek his guidance about whether we should heed the thoughts or perhaps find healing from them.

Keep Spiritual Notes

Many people value journaling as a way to reflect, notice, and review events in their lives. If you enjoy journaling, it is a great way to record your spiritual thoughts and the experiences you have with God.

Recording spiritual notes is similar to journaling. The idea is to keep a notebook on your desk where you can make simple notes about impressions you have in prayer, your spiritual questions, God observations, etc., that happen at work. A sentence or two is all you need to give you a reference to remember.

The notebook acts as a spiritual record, giving you a place to see patterns, reflect on recurring questions, trace themes, remember significant events, and notice how you are growing your connection with God. Reflecting on your notes builds and refines your God knowledge and self knowledge, two key aspects which deepen your relationship with God.

An Invitation to Spiritual Direction

If you want to accelerate your connection with God in your work, or interact with someone to help you process your experiences with the exercises in this workbook, let me introduce you to the ministry of spiritual direction. I have practiced spiritual direction since 2007 and highly recommend this ministry to Christian leaders in both profit and nonprofit settings.

When we are used to doing our work without thinking about or connecting with God it can be difficult to change these habits on our own. Having another person to walk with us on the journey increases our awareness of blind spots and ways we work in auto-pilot. In a similar way that a business coach enriches our leadership skills, a spiritual director assists our connection with God.

A spiritual director is a trained listener who helps you notice both God's presence and activity as well as your personal reactions and responses as you share about what is happening in your life and work. Hospitable and confidential, spiritual direction is a ministry that helps you grow in prayer and live into your calling as a professional and a follower of Christ.

In my experience as a spiritual director, I am amazed at how this hour-a-month investment of time impacts a Christians' awareness of God in their life. After only a few sessions, many people begin to form habits of looking for God's activity in their daily circumstances. They grow to see how their cooperation with what God is doing facilitates spiritual growth.

Benefits of spiritual direction include:

» Identifying blind spots or simple ignorance about how God is using situations to get our attention

» Becoming aware of how we avoid or include God in the choices we make

» The chance to verbally process our lives—name our struggles, admit our feelings, etc.—in a safe environment

» A dialogue partner who asks good questions without judgment or an agenda

» A fellow Christian who desires above all for you to find your deepest fulfillment in your relationship with God

Spiritual direction sessions can happen in person, through video conferencing, or even over the phone. If you would like to learn more about spiritual direction or find a listing of Christian spiritual directors, you can visit Grafted Life Ministries for their association of Christ-centered spiritual directors: *www.graftedlife.org*

If you would like to contact me personally to talk about spiritual direction or to receive help in finding a spiritual director you can email me at *debbie@currentstrategies.com*

Recommended Reading

The following books are good resources to spur your thinking and deepen your understanding of concepts presented in this workbook. If there are other Christians on your team, consider reading and discussing these books together. All titles are available on Amazon.com.

With, by Skye Jethani

With explores the narrative of the Bible to show that we were created to be with God, and that restoring this connection is his mission. Instead of life over, under, from, or even for God, what leads us into freedom and restoration is life with God.

A life lived in rich communion with God cultivates faith, hope, and love in a way that transforms both us and the broken world we inhabit.

Every Good Endeavor, by Timothy Keller

Tim Keller, pastor of New York's Redeemer Presbyterian Church and the New York Times bestselling author of *The Reason for God*, has taught and counseled students, young professionals, and senior leaders on the subject of work and calling for more than twenty years. Now he pulls his insights into a thoughtful and practical book for readers everywhere.

With deep conviction and often surprising advice, Keller shows readers that biblical wisdom is immensely relevant to our questions about work today. In fact, the Christian view of work—that we work to serve others, not ourselves—can provide the foundation of a thriving professional and balanced personal life. Keller shows how excellence, integrity, discipline, creativity, and passion in the workplace can help others and even be considered acts of worship—not just of self-interest.

Pursuing God's Will Together, by Ruth Haley Barton

Meetings can sap our energy, rupture community, and thoroughly demoralize us. They can go on forever with no resolution. Or they can rush along without consensus just to "get through the agenda." What if there was another way?

Church boards and other Christian leadership teams have long relied on models adapted from the business world. Ruth Haley Barton, president of the Transforming Center, helps teams transition to a much more suitable model—the spiritual community that discerns God's will together.

In these pages you will discover personal and group practices that will lead you into a new way of experiencing community and listening to God together.

Do You Love Me? by Debbie Swindoll

What is the quality of your relationship with God? Does it seem close, personal, relevant, and deep? Would you describe it as loving? Or do you operate at a distance from God, unsure about how He really feels about you, or uncertain if you want Him intimately involved in your life?

Do You Love Me? is an invitation to explore your relationship with God and how it affects your life. Debbie Swindoll draws out God's heart for reconciliation and candidly offers examples from her own spiritual journey. This updated edition is designed for individual or group use. It is organized to support your weekly discipleship to Christ with scriptural meditations, discussion questions, and experiential activities.

About the Author

Debbie Swindoll is a spiritual director at heart. She loves to help others grow in awareness of God's presence and their response to God's invitations to be with him in everyday life. As a spiritual integrator at Current Strategies, she consults with Christian leaders as they grow in spiritual awareness, and develops experiences of personal reflection and retreat to help them build deeper relationships with God and their colleagues.

Debbie is the founder of Grafted Life Ministries, a ministry that resources churches interested in developing spiritual relationships and encouraging spiritual growth. She has co-authored 10 formational studies for small groups and published her book *"Do You Love Me? Exploring Our Relationships with God and Others."*

Debbie has an MA in *Spiritual Formation and Soul Care* from Talbot School of Theology at Biola University. She speaks and writes on the intersection of theology, psychology, spirituality, and relational attachment.

Debbie's husband, Curt, is a Certified EOS Implementer® who uses this workbook to help his clients integrate spiritual practices alongside the best practices of EOS.

Debbie can be reached at *debbie@currentstrategies.com*